This Piano Method is respectfully dedicated to my publisher,
Charles Hansen, whose encouragement and guidance made it possible

THE JOHN BRIMHALL PIANO METHOD

THE COMPLETE METHOD of Popular and Traditional Instruction

ISBN 0-8494-2768-1

TEN TIPS FOR QUICK PROGRESS

If, as you practice each new piece, you keep the following points in mind, your practice time will be cut down and your progress increased. These tips will help you to get the most out of each practice session.

1. Observe the Time Signature and the Key Signature, reminding yourself what each means.

2. When beginning a new piece, practice each hand separately. Begin slowly, counting out loud, then gradually increase the speed. Put both hands together. Begin slowly, counting out loud, then gradually increased the speed.

3. Observe everything carefully as you play — notes, fingering, rests, phrasing, expression marks. Remember, if you don't make a mistake you won't have to spend your time going back to correct it.

4. When you do make a mistake, correct it immediately, before going on. Don't practice mistakes. You learn by building a habit of doing it right!

5. When you have to stop, begin again at the beginning of a phrase. Remember that a phrase is a musical sentence.

6. Isolate difficult sections, practicing them until you have conquered them, rather than stumbling over them every time you go through the piece.

7. Keep in mind as you play the piano that you are playing three things at once — Melody, Bass Line and Harmonic Accompaniment. Try to keep each in its proper place. The best way to make one hand sound louder is to play the other hand softer.

8. The way to build your memory is to start memorizing from the beginning. Pick out occasional pieces that you enjoy playing and memorize them, reviewing them every week or so. Don't wait until you get to the more difficult pieces before you begin memorizing.

9. Play your exercises faithfully and carefully, so that when you are ready for more advanced pieces, your fingers will be ready, too.

10. No matter what kind of music you play, from Beethoven to Boogie Woogie, it is attention to detail and accuracy of rhythm that makes one player sound better than another. For maximum enjoyment and results, *"Do it right"* from the beginning.

7987

TO THE TEACHER

The John Brimhall Piano Method is a complete method. In addition to the standard and traditional technic, theory, folk music and classical piano literature, it contains the elements of standard technique and a liberal collection of the best of familiar music. This method contains a broad musical library of universal interest.

It is hoped that students using the books in this method will develop an understanding and a love of the classics, while their interest is maintained at the highest level through the study of the familiar music that they hear on radio and television.

New material is introduced gradually throughout the series, through reading, not playing by ear. After a student reads competently, improvisation is taught, but always solidly grounded in theory. By careful attention to detail the student should build accurate and musical habits that will carry over into any music he plays.

THE JOHN BRIMHALL PIANO METHOD

Book 1

FUNDAMENTALS OF MUSIC

THE STAFF

Notes are written on the lines and spaces of the STAFF.

Piano music uses a TREBLE STAFF for high notes.

TREBLE (OR G) CLEF

and a BASS STAFF for low notes.

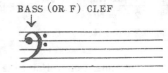

BASS (OR F) CLEF

When these two staffs are joined together by a brace, the result is called a GREAT STAFF. The high notes are written toward the top, the low notes are written toward the bottom.

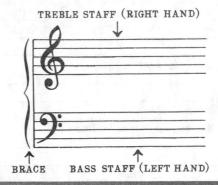

TREBLE STAFF (RIGHT HAND)

BRACE   BASS STAFF (LEFT HAND)

KEYBOARD CHART

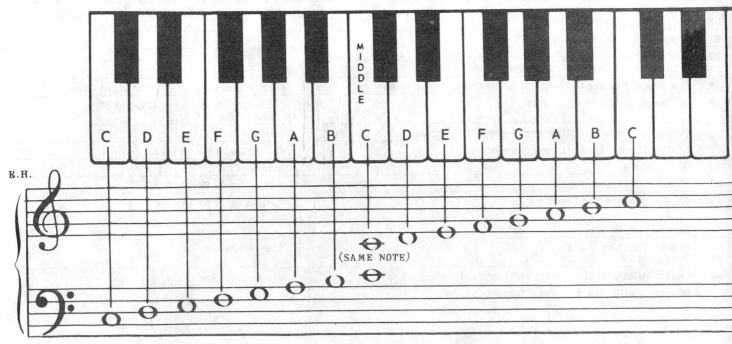

MEASURES

BEATS are grouped together to form measures. MEASURES may contain two, three, four or more beats.

Measures are separated by BAR LINES.

The end of a composition is indicated by a DOUBLE BAR.

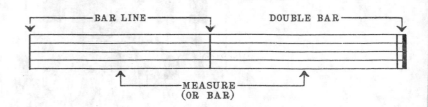

TIME SIGNATURE

The grouping of beats into measures is indicated by the TIME SIGNATURE, which appears at the beginning of each composition. The top number of the time signature tells how many beats there are in each measure. The bottom number tells what kind of note is to receive one beat or count.

$$\frac{4}{4} = \begin{array}{l} \text{4 beats in each measure.} \\ \text{Each quarter note (} \textstyle\bullet\!\!\!\!\text{ }) \text{ gets one beat.} \end{array}$$

Quarter note   (♩) = 1 beat

Half note   (♩) = 2 beats

Whole note   (o) = 4 beats

At first you should clap or tap out the rhythm of each new piece, while counting out loud. As you begin to play each piece on the piano, continue to count out loud. This will help you to build solid rhythm, which is the foundation of good playing.

THE HANDS

Numbers are placed near the notes to tell you which fingers to use. The fingers are numbered like this:

The hands must be slightly cupped, so that the fingers are rounded and strike the keys with the soft pad at the tip of the finger. The thumb must also be rounded so that it strikes the key with the soft pad at the outside of the nail.

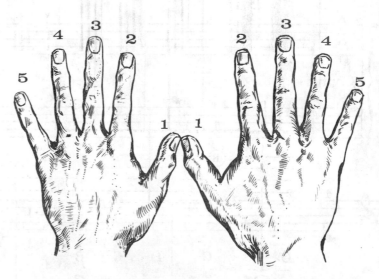

LEFT HAND   RIGHT HAND

FIRST HAND POSITION
BOTH THUMBS ARE ON MIDDLE C

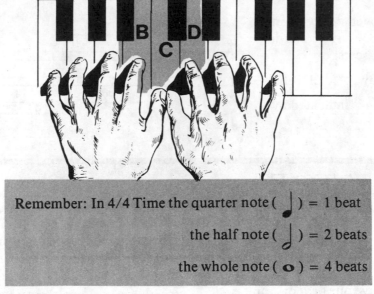

Remember: In 4/4 Time the quarter note (♩) = 1 beat

the half note (♩) = 2 beats

the whole note (o) = 4 beats

ON MIDDLE C

Remember To Count Out Loud!

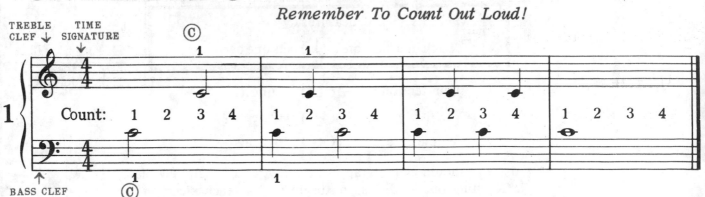

TWO NEW NOTES

THREE NOTE TUNE

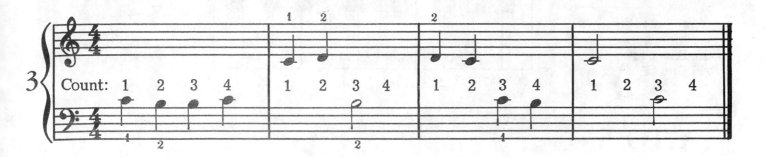

AROUND MIDDLE C

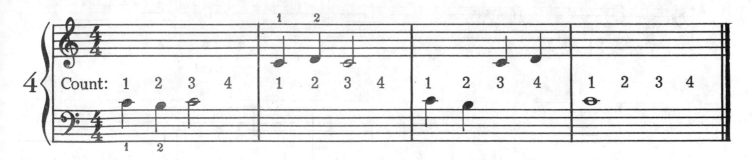

C - D - B - C

8

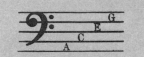
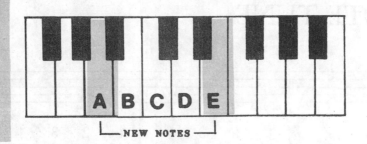

NEW NOTES

A TO E

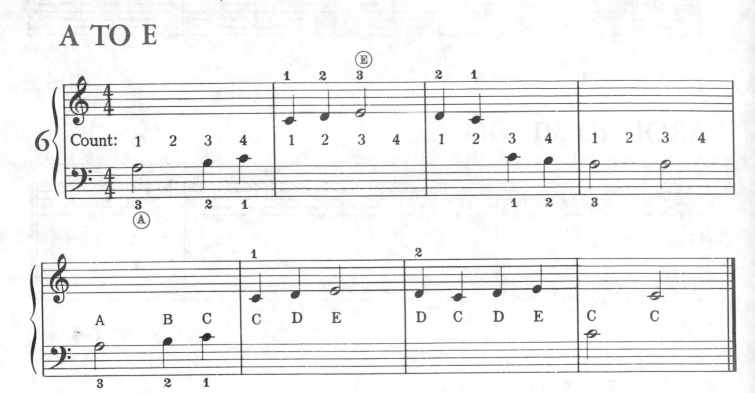

FIRST DANCE

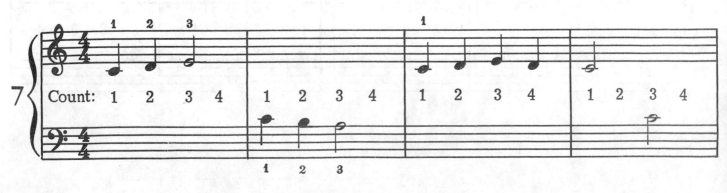

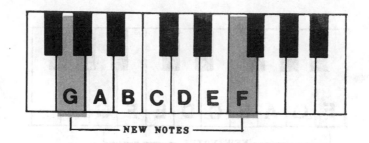

NEW NOTES

TWO MORE NEW NOTES

TOE-HEEL DANCE

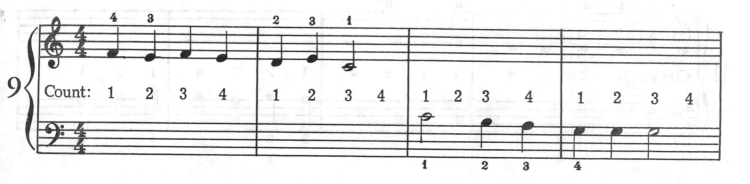

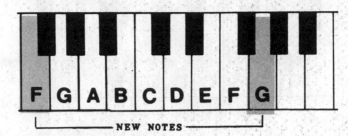

ALL FIVE FINGERS

FIRST EXERCISE

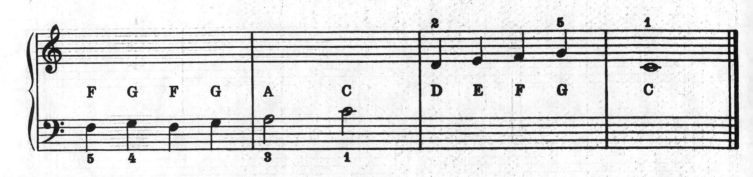

3	3 beats in each measure.
4	Each quarter note (♩) gets one beat.

Quarter note	(♩)	= 1 beat
Half note	(♩)	= 2 beats
Dotted half note	(♩.)	= 3 beats

ONE, TWO, THREE

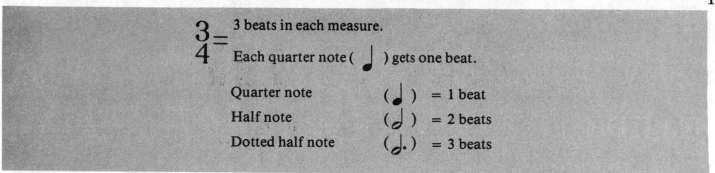

WALTZ TUNE

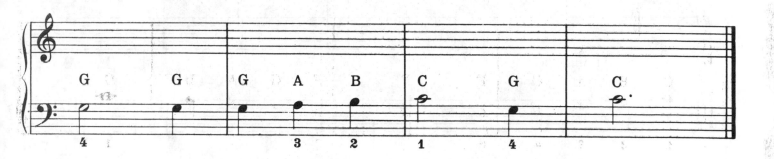
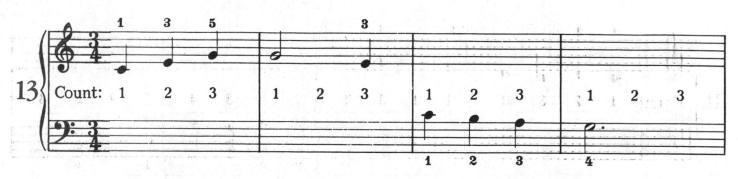
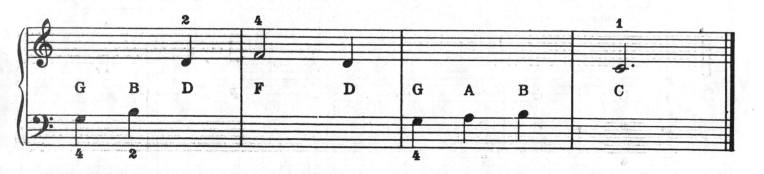

RESTS

A REST is a symbol for a definite time value of silence.

Whole measure rest . . . . ▬ = 𝅝 . . . . . . Whole note (4 beats)

Half rest . . . . ▬ = 𝅗𝅥 . . . . Half note (2 beats)

Quarter rest . . . . 𝄽 = 𝅘𝅥 . . . . . Quarter note (1 beat)

In these pieces, for the first time in this book, two notes are played together. Make sure they sound at exactly the same time. Practice each hand separately, counting out loud. Then put the two hands together.

AIR FROM "MARTHA"

FRIEDERICH von FLOTOW

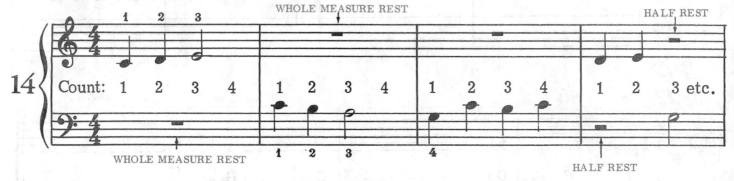

FIRST HARMONY

In a piece in which both hands play at the same time, it is a good idea to practice each hand separately, before playing them together. Remember to count carefully.

STUDY IN HARMONY

BOTH HANDS

SLURS

A SLUR is a curved line over or under a group of notes. It is a phrase mark, telling the player to play the slurred notes in a smooth and connected manner. The Italian musical term is LEGATO.

To play legato, each piano key should not be allowed to rise until the following one is struck. Do not allow the sounds to blur together, but listen for a smooth and clean connection between the notes. In the case of repeated notes within a legato phrase, be careful to make as little break between them as possible.

PROGRESS

ETUDE (Etude is French for Study or Exercise)

FIVE FINGER POSITION– C MAJOR

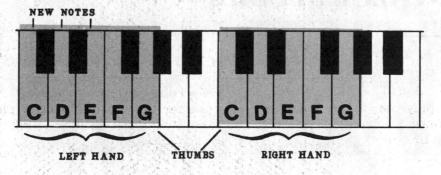

FIRST SCALE STUDY

20

EXERCISE IN CONTRARY MOTION

21

NOTE-VALUE STUDIES

1 whole note . . . . 𝅝 = ♩♩♩♩ . . . . 4 quarter notes

1 dotted half note . . . . 𝅗𝅥. = ♩♩♩ . . . . 3 quarter notes

1 half note. . . . . 𝅗𝅥 = ♩♩ . . . . 2 quarter notes

FOUR NOTES TO ONE

Don't Forget To Practice Each Hand Separately, Counting Out Loud.

SWINGING

TWO NOTES TO ONE

THE VILLAGE BAND

CARL CZERNY

ONE NOTE TO ONE

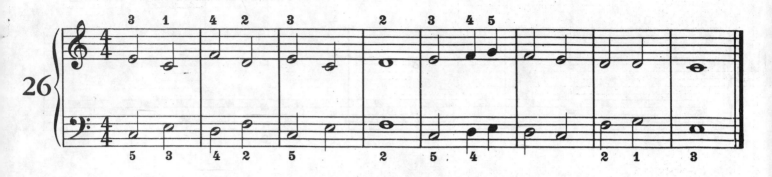

STUDY

CARL CZERNY

MINIATURE MARCH

CARL CZERNY

THREE NOTES TO ONE

WALTZ AROUND

A SUMMER DAY

FERDINAND BEYER

MELODY AND ACCOMPANIMENT

The MELODY is the tune, or leading part of a composition. In a song, the melody is sung by adding words to it. The melody is made up of one note at a time. The rest of the notes are the ACCOMPANIMENT, so called because it goes along with or accompanies the melody. The accompaniment may contain a harmony part made up of chords, bass line or counter-melody, or it may contain all three.

Always remember that the melody is more important than the accompaniment. Therefore, play the accompaniment a little softer than the melody, so the melody will stand out more clearly.

LIGHTLY ROW

TRADITIONAL

INTERVALS

An INTERVAL is the distance between two notes. The number size of an interval is figured by counting the total number of letter names the interval includes. Always count UP the alphabet.

C-D includes only two letters of the alphabet, C and D, so the interval is a 2nd.

D-F includes three letters of the alphabet, D, E and F, so the interval is a 3rd.

A-G includes seven letters of the alphabet, A,B,C,D,E,F and G, so the interval is a 7th.

Here are some more examples.

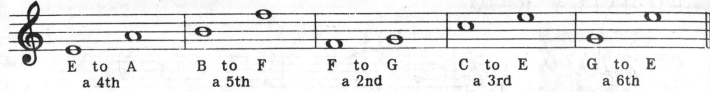

| E to A | B to F | F to G | C to E | G to E |
| a 4th | a 5th | a 2nd | a 3rd | a 6th |

An interval which appears one note at a time, is called a MELODIC INTERVAL.

An interval of two notes, played at the same time, is called a HARMONIC INTERVAL.

INTERVALS FOR RIGHT HAND
MAKE SURE THAT BOTH NOTES SOUND EXACTLY TOGETHER

INTERVALS FOR LEFT HAND

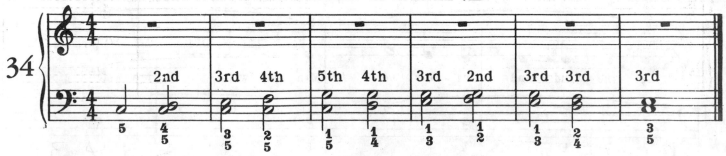

MELODIC INTERVAL EXERCISE

THE TIE

A TIE is a curved line connecting two notes of the same pitch. The first note is played and held for the combined total count of the two notes, without re-striking the note.

A tie is necessary if you wish to hold a note beyond the bar line. The tie in this illustration creates a note of six counts, which would otherwise be impossible in 3/4 time.

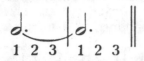

SUMMER BREEZE

By JOHN BRIMHALL

CHORDS

A CHORD is a combination of musical tones.

A chord may be played SOLID (all at once) 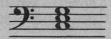 or BROKEN (one note at a time)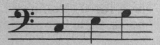

C MAJOR CHORD (C)

LEFT HAND  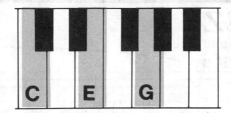 RIGHT HAND

C MAJOR CHORD STUDY

Note: A WHOLE MEASURE REST (——) gets 3 beats in 3/4 time.

G SEVENTH CHORD (G7)

LEFT HAND  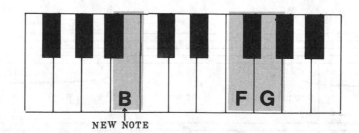 RIGHT HAND

NEW NOTE

G SEVENTH CHORD STUDY

THE WALTZ

The WALTZ is a dance in 3/4 time. It developed in Austria and Germany in the late 18th Century, and soon spread through the rest of the Western World. Vienna was the center of the development of the waltz. Johann Strauss, composer of *"The Blue Danube"* is the most famous composer of Viennese Waltzes.

WALTZ ON THE C CHORD

Remember: A QUARTER REST (𝄽) gets one beat.

LITTLE WALTZ

Make a contrast between the loud and soft playing in this piece.
Remember- *p* = soft, *mp* = medium soft, *f* = loud.

CARL CZERNY

*This kind of double bar means the end of a section, but not the end of the whole composition.

The CHORD SYMBOLS (C and G7) have been added to the music of *"Little Waltz."* These symbols are musical shorthand telling which chord harmonizes with the melody. Try playing the right hand part of *"Little Waltz"* with the solid forms of the C and G7 chords which were presented on page 24, instead of playing the written left hand part.

REPEAT SIGN

These are REPEAT SIGNS. They indicate that the measures between them are to played twice.

In "*Some Folks,*" the repeat signs indicate that the entire song is to be repeated. Both of the songs on this page are accompanied by the two chords (C and G7) that you have already learned.

SOME FOLKS

STEPHEN FOSTER

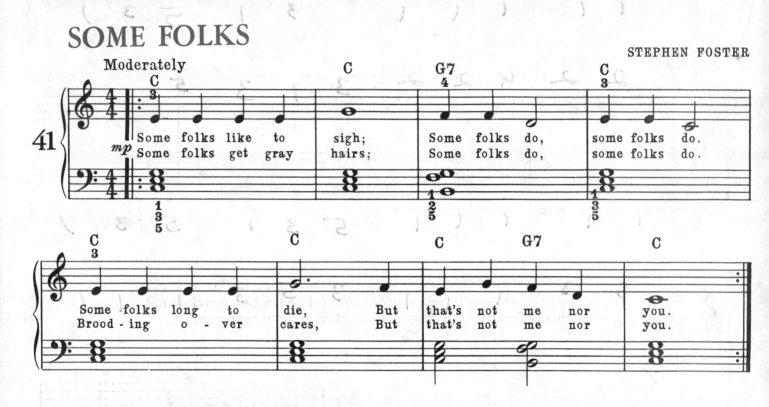

SYMPHONIC THEME

LUDWIG VAN BEETHOVEN

F CHORD (F)

LEFT HAND

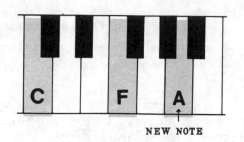

NEW NOTE

RIGHT HAND

F CHORD STUDY

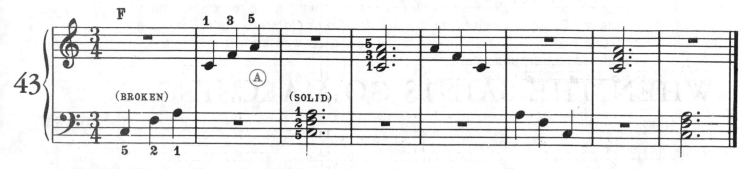

THREE CHORDS (PRINCIPAL CHORDS IN C MAJOR)

Many songs can be harmonized using the three chords in this exercise, particularly folk songs and easy popular songs. Practice this exercise until you can change freely from one chord to another, without hesitation.

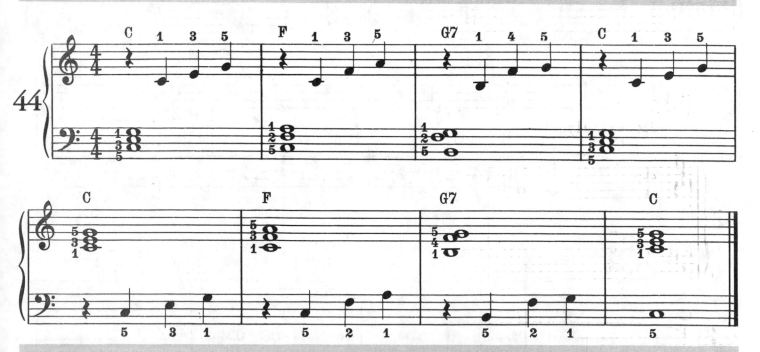

POPULAR MUSIC literally means the "music of the people." In our time it has come to mean the lighter types of recorded and broadcast music, including popular songs, rock and roll, country-western music, soul music, and many other varieties. Some of the music of the great composers such as Mozart and Beethoven were the "popular music" of their day.

PICK-UP

Some pieces do not begin on the first beat of the measure. If a piece begins with only part of a measure, this part is called a PICK-UP. When there is a pick-up, there must be a partial measure at the end of the piece, to complete the measure of the pick-up.

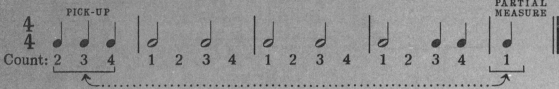

The word "Traditional" at the top right side of the music means no one knows who wrote the song. It was passed on from person to person until someone finally wrote it down. *"When The Saints Go Marching In"* is one of the most widely known traditional songs, so well known that it has achieved popular song status.

WHEN THE SAINTS GO MARCHING IN

TRADITIONAL

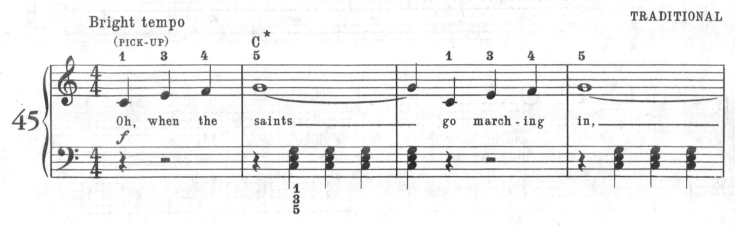

* It is customary to add the chord symbol only where the chord changes.

When The Saints Go Marching In-2-2

SHARP

♯ A SHARP is a sign which indicates that a note is to be played 1/2 step higher.

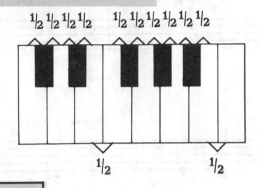

The entire piano keyboard is made up of HALF STEPS.

Therefore, a sharp is played on the very next key to the right. (1/2 step higher)

If a sharp appears in front of an F, instead of playing the white key, F, play the black key to its right, F sharp.

WHOLE STEP

A WHOLE STEP is composed of two half steps.

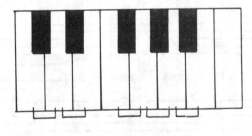

WHOLE STEPS

WHOLE STEPS

In all of these whole steps, we have skipped over the black key in between. Whole steps may also be from black key to white key, white key to black key, or black key to black key, just so one key is skipped in between.

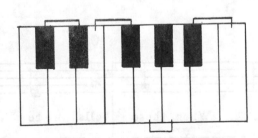

SCALE

A SCALE is a series of notes in succession. The MAJOR SCALE is the most common scale. It is built of two whole steps, one half step, three whole steps and one half step.

C MAJOR SCALE

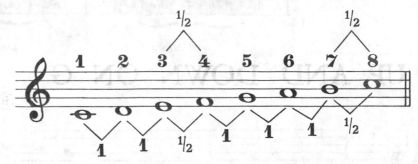

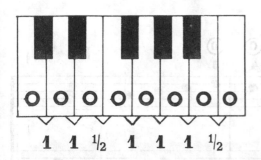

There is a half step between the 3rd and 4th, and between the 7th and 8th notes of the major scale.

Since this major scale pattern was started on C, it is called the C Major Scale. Major scales may be started on any note, but must always be built with the major scale pattern of steps and half steps.

$$(1 - 1 - \tfrac{1}{2} - 1 - 1 - 1 - \tfrac{1}{2}).$$

G MAJOR SCALE

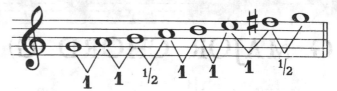

Here is a Major Scale Pattern built on G.

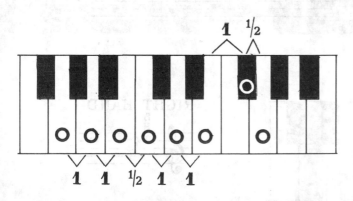

Since this major scale pattern was started on G, it is called the G Major Scale. The G Major Scale has one sharp, F sharp, so the Key of G Major has one sharp, F sharp.

KEY SIGNATURE

Up to this point, all of the pieces in this book have been in the KEY OF C MAJOR, which has no sharps.

The KEY SIGNATURE is placed at the beginning of each line of music, to tell which key you are in, and which sharps should be played.

KEY OF C MAJOR
No sharps

KEY OF G MAJOR
1 sharp—F♯

FIVE FINGER POSITION- G MAJOR

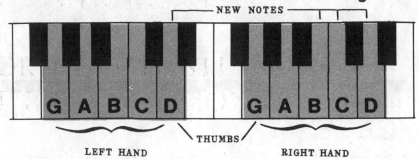

NEW NOTES

G A B C D   G A B C D

LEFT HAND   THUMBS   RIGHT HAND

UP AND DOWN ON G

A LEGER LINE is a short line, added above or below a staff. You have been playing Middle C, which is always on a leger line. Now, in the Five Finger Position in G Major, you will learn two new leger line notes.

SAME NOTES in 𝄞 and 𝄢

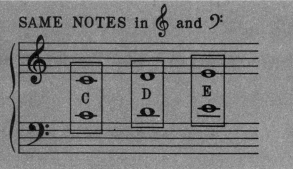

C   D   E

G MAJOR CHORD (G)

LEFT HAND

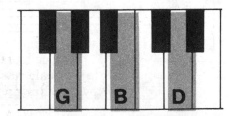

G   B   D

RIGHT HAND

G MAJOR CHORD STUDY

D SEVENTH CHORD (D7)

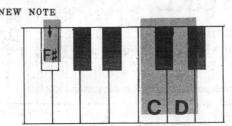

D SEVENTH CHORD STUDY

C CHORD (C)

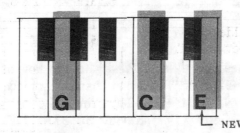

C CHORD STUDY

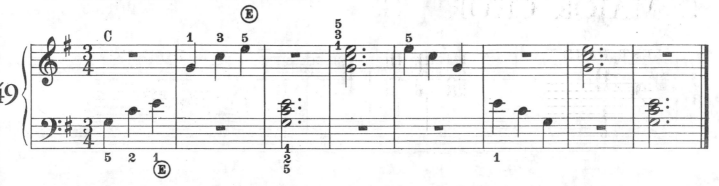

THREE CHORDS IN G MAJOR

PRINCIPAL CHORDS

The chords built on the first (I), fourth (IV) and fifth (V) steps of the scale are called the PRINCIPAL CHORDS of a key. The principal chords of the key of C Major are C (I), F (IV) and G7 (V7). Review No. 31.

LITTLE PIECE

ANTONIO DIABELLI

Now that you have learned *"Little Piece"* in the key of C Major, play No.39B, in the key of G Major. The act of changing a piece from one key to another is called TRANSPOSITION. The principal chords of the key of G Major are G (I), C (IV) and D7 (V7). Review No. 37.

LITTLE PIECE

ANTONIO DIABELLI

Now that you have read a piece that has been transposed from C Major to G Major, go back and transpose No. 28, No. 29 and No. 32 into the key of G Major. Transpose by using a change of hand position. Remember: G Major has one sharp, F sharp.

BROKEN CHORDS

In this song, a variety of BROKEN CHORD is used.

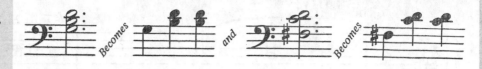

Remember: In the Key of G Major all F's are to be played as F#'s.

DU, DU LIEGST MIR IM HERZEN

GERMAN SONG

MODERATO (Moderate Speed)

*Play the 2nd finger, then bring the Thumb UNDER for the next note.

IN MAY

By FRANZ BEHR

EIGHTH NOTE

♪ is an EIGHTH NOTE. When two eighth notes appear together, they are written like this: ♫ = ♩

Two eighth notes equal one quarter note and are played evenly in one beat. ♫ = ♩

❜ is an EIGHTH REST. It has the same value as an eighth note.

Until you are more familiar with eighth notes, count:

1 & 2 & 3 & 4 &

Later, when you can feel the division of the beat into two parts, count:

1 2 3 4

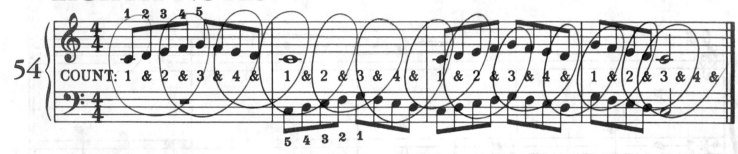

EIGHTH NOTES

COUNT: 1 & 2 & 3 & 4 & | 1 & 2 & 3 & 4 & | 1 & 2 & 3 & 4 & | 1 & 2 & 3 & 4 &

BOOGIE BEAT

JOHN BRIMHALL

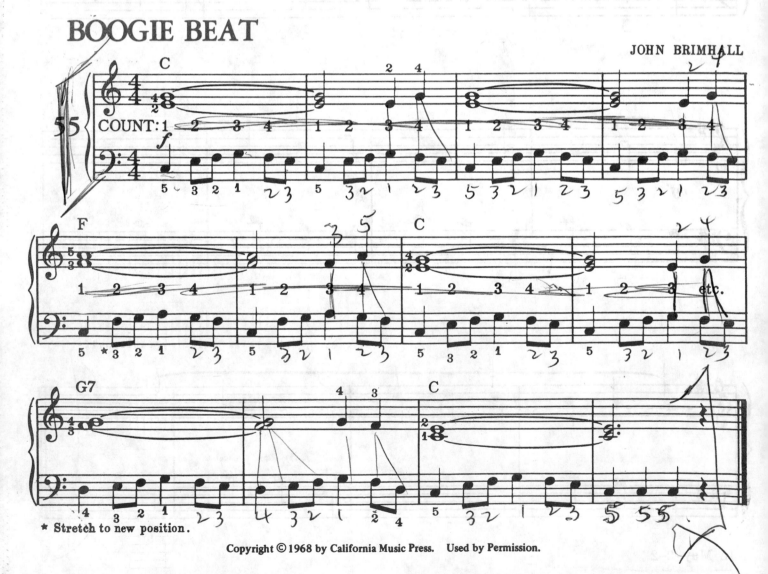

COUNT: 1 2 3 4 | 1 2 3 4 | 1 2 3 4 | 1 2 3 4

* Stretch to new position.

FOLK DANCE

"This Old Man" begins in a new position for the right hand. Place the 4th finger on G. In the 5th measure, the right hand stretches back to the Five Finger Position, with the thumb on Middle C.

THIS OLD MAN

TRADITIONAL

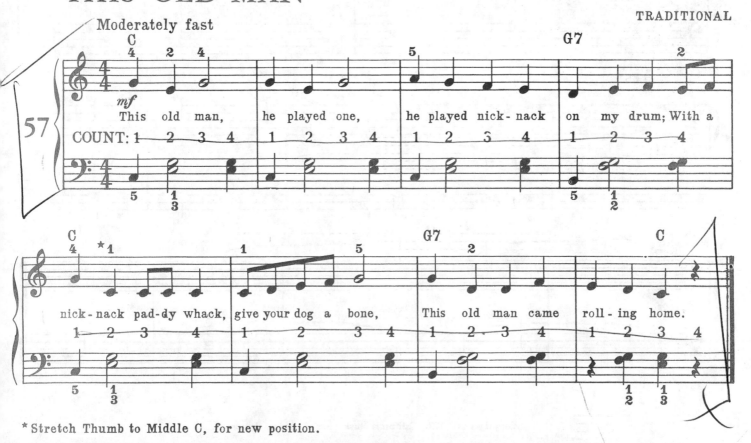

This old man, he played one, he played nick-nack on my drum; With a

nick-nack pad-dy whack, give your dog a bone, This old man came roll-ing home.

* Stretch Thumb to Middle C, for new position.

♮ is a NATURAL. It cancels a sharp or a flat.

A sharp or natural that appears in the body of a song, rather than in the key signature is called an ACCIDENTAL. It is only in effect for the measure in which it appears and is cancelled by the next bar line. Sometimes, an unnecessary accidental is placed in parenthesis, as a reminder. Look at measures 8 and 13.

SECOND PART (𝄢 Accompaniment)

REVERIE

By JOHN BRIMHALL

A DUET is played by two persons at the same piano. One plays in the treble clef while the other plays in the bass clef. Traditionally, the treble clef part has the melody while the bass clef part has the accompaniment. Take turns playing both parts with your teacher or with another student. In the bass part, watch for the changes of left hand position, due to the sharps and naturals. In the treble part, watch for changes of position throughout the piece. At first, practice each hand separately.

FIRST PART (𝄞 Melody)

REVERIE

By JOHN BRIMHALL

* Move hand to new position

The words of Guantanamera were written by Cuba's national poet, Jose Marti, who died in the Cuban struggle for independence from Spain in 1895. Freely translated, the words mean: I am a sincere man from where the palms grow. Before I die I would like to speak the poems of my soul. The melody dates from the Seventeenth Century and was later joined to the Marti words.

GUANTANAMERA
(LADY OF GUANTANAMO)

TRADITIONAL CUBAN MELODY

* The dotted line shows the movement of the melody from hand to hand.

SCARBOROUGH FAIR

This arrangement is in a five finger pattern. Place the left thumb on Middle C and the right thumb on D. Each hand covers five keys and does not move from its original position.

16th Century English Folk Song

Moderately

SIGNS AND SYMBOLS

p   (piano) — soft

mp   (mezzo piano) — moderately soft

mf   (mezzo forte) — moderately loud

f   (forte) — loud

𝄞   Treble Clef

𝄢   Bass Clef

𝄆 𝄇   Repeat Signs

♯   Sharp — Raises the pitch of a note 1/2 step.

8va-   Play one octave higher than written.

C   Common Time (same as 4/4 Time)

>   Accent — Give added emphasis

☰   Staff

DICTIONARY OF TERMS

Allegro: Cheerful, quick.

Chord: Combination of notes.

Great Staff: Treble Staff and Bass Staff joined together. Used for piano music.

Legato: Smooth and connected.

Moderato: Moderate speed.

Pickup: A partial measure at the beginning of a piece.

Staccato: Short, detached. (opposite of legato)

Transposition: The act of changing a piece to a different key.

Triad: A three note chord.

TIME SIGNATURES

$\frac{3}{4}$ 3 beats in each measure

Each quarter note gets one beat

$\frac{4}{4}$ 4 beats in each measure

Each quarter note gets one beat

NOTES AND RESTS

Note	Note Name	Beats in 2/4, 3/4 or 4/4 Time	Rest	Rest Name
𝅝	Whole Note	4	▬	Whole Measure Rest
𝅗𝅥.	Dotted Half Note	3		
𝅗𝅥	Half Note	2	▬	Half Rest
♩	Quarter Note	1	𝄽	Quarter Rest
♪	Eighth Note	½	𝄾	Eighth Rest

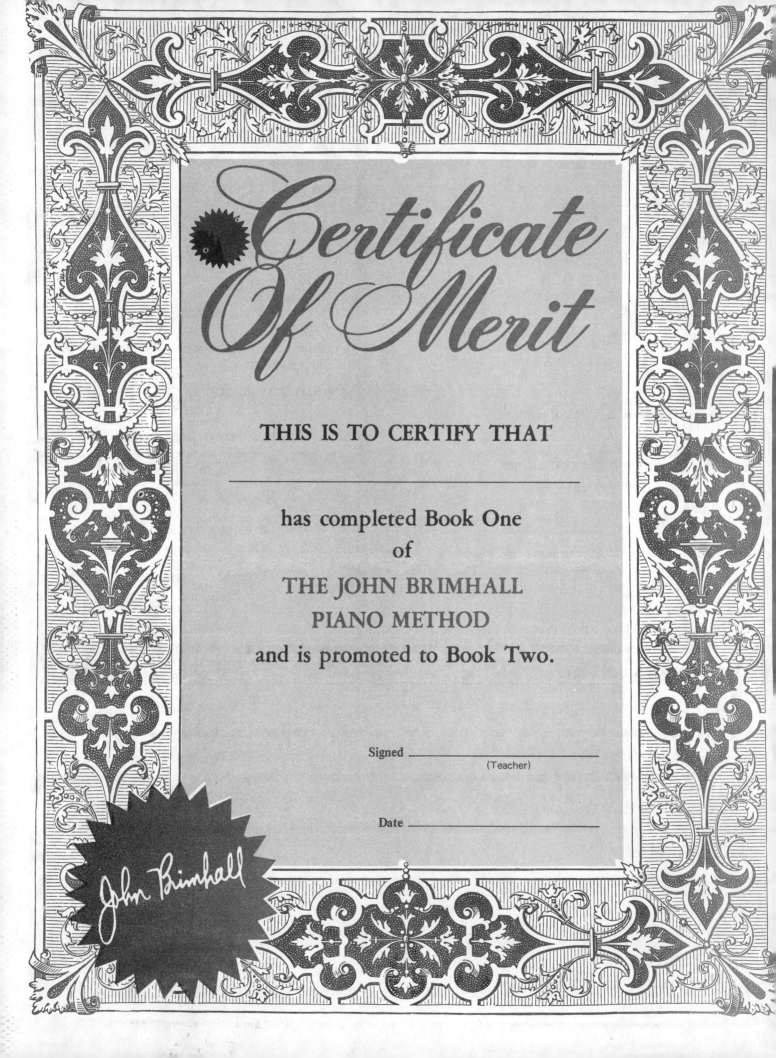

Certificate Of Merit

THIS IS TO CERTIFY THAT

_____

has completed Book One

of

THE JOHN BRIMHALL

PIANO METHOD

and is promoted to Book Two.

Signed _____
(Teacher)

Date _____

John Brimhall